3 Decades Later: Experiencing the 30th Year
THE ADDENDUM

Copyright © 2019 by Beverly Morrison Caesar

Requests for information should be directed to:
ZizaCreative Publishing, Inc.
718.708.3348 | RaseacInc@gmail.com
New York

Cover Design by Alvida Carter
Interior Design by ZizaCreative Publishing, Inc.

All scripture references are taken from the King James Bible unless otherwise indicated. All doctrinal beliefs expressed in this story are those of the author exclusively and do not necessarily express the views of ZizaCreative Publishing, Inc.

Printed in the United States of America
Second printing edition

ISBN: 978-0-578-50619-7

BEVERLY MORRISON CAESAR

THREE DECADES
LATER

EXPERIENCING THE 30TH YEAR - THE ADDENDUM

DEDICATION

This book is dedicated to my husband whose support and encouragement pushed me toward my destiny and my purpose. A huge shout-out to my three daughters - Naomi, Lydia and Elizabeth who constantly nudged me to reach for the stars! I also dedicate this book to our grand children, Kayliah, Selah and Roderick IV. May they grow to appreciate the Almighty, Miracle Working God in a profound way. The legacy lives on through them.

SPECIAL THANKS

Alvida Carter, Naomi Caesar Hunter, Ismay Phillips, Karlene Thompson, Frederick Towles and Vivian Nero

"Faith does not eliminate questions.
But faith knows where to take them."
-Elisabeth Elliot

TABLE OF CONTENTS

FOREWORD

Recently, a store display of small glass vases caught our attention. The containers held unopened flower bulbs in water. Through the clear glass you could see the dark bulb inside, with its noodle-like roots proceeding downward, and green stalks shooting upward. No flowers were yet to be found—except on the attached photo tag.

We brought one of the vases home. The tag informed us it was a "Pink Hyacinth." It looked so interesting, even if it didn't exactly resemble the photo. It was placed upon a table.

Did it take just a matter of hours—maybe a day or two? Whatever the time frame, it was a rapid transformation! We were amazed at the speedy emergence of beautiful pink flowers, and how forcefully the flowers reached upward and outward from the little glass container.

In her previous book, *Experiencing the 25th Hour*, Pastor Beverly Caesar allowed us to 'see through the glass' of personal and family experiences that were very challenging. And yet, through those pages, we were reminded that when the LORD provides a faith rooted in His Word, His suffering people can look up high in the hope of His promises.

Now, in *Experiencing the 30th Year*, we are again invited to rejoice in the miracle-working and promise-keeping God! Because the severely at-risk baby we met in the previous book is now Pastor Rod Caesar III, the Senior Pastor of Bethel Gospel Tabernacle. Three decades after medical professionals doubted he would survive infancy, Pastor Rod is pointing others to the Savior of sinners, the Lord Jesus Christ.

Psalm 77:14 says, "You are the God who works wonders; you have made known your might among the peoples." (ESV). God is still performing wonders in and through the life of Pastor Rod—and I believe the best is yet to come.

So, let's 'look through the glass' in the following pages...and let's continue to give the God of wonders all the glory!

Pastor Stephen Samuel,
Westbury Gospel Tabernacle, NY

> *"Change will not come if we wait*
> *for some other person or some other time.*
> *We are the ones we've been waiting for.*
> *We are the change that we seek."*
> **–President Barack Obama–**

PROLOGUE

Having written the memoir, *Experiencing the 25th Hour* about 19 years ago, and receiving numerous amazing testimonies from readers, I though it was time for my husband and me to bring everyone up to date on Roderick III.

With my busy schedule and time restraints I wondered if it would be possible to accomplish this undertaking. My hands are full:

- Owning and operating a publishing company - ZizaCreative Inc.

- Running a theatrical training and production company - Arts in Christian Theatre Inc. and ACTStudios.

- Supervising a newly formed W.I.V.E.S. Forum.

- Maintaining my pastoral duties at BethelGT.

- Ensuring that Bishop and I support our branch churches in Long Island, Brooklyn, Conyers, GA, Haiti & the Caribbean.

With the support of my husband and knowing that time was of the essence, I did my best to press through. I was determined by the grace of God to ensure completion of this addendum so that our readers could be updated, at least by Rod's 30th birthday.

❧ ☙

Although this addendum is about Rod III, he couldn't have made it to this moment in time if it had not been for some important people in his life. Aside from us - his parents, our first born Naomi who, when Rod was a baby, was on hand to protect him from situations that could have cost him his life, as you will read in *Experiencing the 25th Hour.* On more than one occasions her careful attention to his well being saved his life from certain death! She was an imaginative eight year old big sister who assumed the role of an attentive "mother hen." Her protection of her baby brother was unshakable. Her watchful eye was one of concern and care. Because she was so responsible the nurses and I trusted her to assist us in his care.

Today, married to Brian Hunter, she serves with her brother as part of his pastoral lead team and on the publication, promotional and graphic teams of BethelGT. She continues to be an asset to her brother. Naomi recognizes her role as she assists him without being overbearing and pushy. Her little brother has matured and stepped into his divine purpose and she watched it unfold - up close and personal.

He values her advice and her carefully processed opinions. I am godly proud to see them working together in ministry.

Lydia, our second born was a precocious child when Rod was born. "Mischievousness" was her middle name. Curiosity and inquisitiveness were her constant companions. Additionally, she was stubborn and strong willed. I remember having to read James Dobson's book, *The Strong Willed Child* in order to keep her in check. Believe me when I tell you - it helped!!

She had to learn the value of safety around her "sickly" brother, and on occasion I allowed her to assist in changing his breathing tube. That would "make her day." I shared in my previous book how Satan attempted to kill her and at the time, her 10-month old daughter, my first granddaughter, Kayliah, in a car accident. I will never forgot that day in May, around my birthday, when God showed us another miracle of preserving and protecting two lives!!

Today, although living in another state and married to Wayne Adams, I admire their continual sibling relationships. Lydia, is only a phone call away and is willing, with the blessings and support of her husband to even serve Bethel on the missions field and in any area of ministry. Her brother is thankful for the assurance in knowing that she too, understands his call and supports him implicitly.

⚜

Although Elizabeth (Beth) came on the scene when Rod was about three years old, the bond between them was and continues to be remarkable. This fourth child was an unexpected blessing who has brought joy to our family and added a new level of creativity to our already creative family! She and her brother became play mates, best friends and "running buddies." As their chauffeur, the YMCA, swimming, gymnastics, music, voice lessons and other activities became our weekly routine. They were inseparable. Rod protecting Beth and Beth trying to keep up with him. It was a joy watching them grow up together. Naomi and Lydia were a pair and Rod and Beth - the other pair.

I am still waiting on the verdict concerning God's plans to unfold for Beth to serve along-side her brother! She is musically gifted, a creative lyricist, dramatically intuitive and loves the Lord passionately. She's ready to roll up her sleeves to ensure the success of this ministry which is a part of her legacy. God is a masterful visionary and an awesome family planner. Who wouldn't serve this omniscient Creator!

⚜

His aunts, Beverly Sherrod and Sandra Hollingsworth had "hands on care" in attending to Rod during the critical developmental years of his life. They offered relief when Roderick and I needed to get out of the house, go to the movies, go for a drive or have a relaxing dinner at one of our favorite restaurants. Aunt Sandra, as a RN would often-times be his nurse on duty.

Today his Aunt, Pastor Beverly Caesar Sherrod serves alongside him in ministry on the pastoral front line team. Lending oversight to the counseling ministry and to the Bible Institute help to strengthen their bond. She helps to lighten his many responsibilities by undertaking the task of scheduling Bethel's activities, programs, meetings and special events, ensuring that all the nuts and bolts are in place. Observing nephew and aunt working closely together warms my heart knowing that his proud aunt recognizes and honors the mantle on his life. She respects his office and encourages him often. I'm sure his grandparents, Roderick Sr. and Gertrude are smiling from heaven resting assuredly that Bethel is in good hands.

His cousin Rhonda was also available in offering assistance, even babysitting all three children, when we needed a break. That was a major undertaking! I would often-times tell Rhonda that she had wisdom "beyond her years." She looked after them with cautious and careful parental care so much so one would think she was their mother! Today she serves as one of the ministers in the BethelGT organization holding up the hands of her cousin. As a prayer intercessor I know she's keeping her dialogue open with God where Pastor Rod is concerned. Kudos to you Rhonda.

A pivotal person in his life is his godmother Robyn Edwards - affectionately called "Auntie." Robyn, although not sisters by birth, is considered my little sister as I took her under my wings at the tender and susceptible age of 14. We raised her as part of the family, so in essence she is just that!

When Rod was born, I decided to make her a godmother, and believe me when I tell you, that was the best decision I could have made. She has taken the role seriously and from day one until today she has poured into his life as if she birthed him! When I needed to sleep, she was right there allowing me to sleep without disturbance for as long as I needed. God has a sense of humor, in that, during her teenage, adolescence and early adult years I was her big sister and mentor. Today, she's a pastor, overseer and pastoral coach. Our roles changed and now she's the best mentor and coach not only to me but to Rod III as well. What a blessing she has been and continues to be to him, to the Caesar family, and to BethelGT.

<hr />

Thelma Harty is another godmother who took on the role diligently and seriously. As a baby with a tracheotomy, underdeveloped lungs, paralyzed vocal cords and other developmental issues, Thelma was a "nurse sent by God." Since he needed round the clock medical care and medical attention, Thelma, on many occasions would fill in when the nursing pool was low. Many times I needed rest and she would show up just in time to give me the sleep relief that my tired body yearned for. She doted on us by continually blessing us with dinners, groceries, toiletries and clothing.

Today she's still serving and graciously extending herself to her god-son in ways too numerous to count. She continues to serve his family. You would think that she knew Stefanie (Rod's wife) all her life. She embraced her with open arms and continually dotes on Stef, Rod and the children. She's an angel "undercover." Only eternity will show the overwhelming graciousness and love she extended to the Caesar family.

Grandmommy (my mom - Mommy) although she lived out of state made it her joyful duty to serve my family with honor and distinction. Her prayers were full of hope and she thought it not robbery to cook, clean, do laundry and run the house for us. When I got pregnant with Beth and was put on monitored bed rest she was there! When Beth came into the world at nine pounds Mommy took Rod III to Maryland and looked after him for about six months enabling me to "catch my breath." My mother was a stalwart and faithful woman of God.

Although I very seldom heard her say, "I love you" her actions displayed her sacrificial and genuine love to us. Today her prayers live on through her grand son. I'm sure as she watches from heaven, smiles break across her face as her heart becomes glad knowing that he's fulfilling his destiny.

Grandma Myrtle, who is now in glory was a heroine in her own right. Having raised Roderick Jr. and Beverly - Bishop Sr. and Gertrude's children - she took on the role of a surrogate grandmother to Rod III. She extended herself as the official family photographer, occasional babysitter, assistant housekeeper and chauffeur. Her memory lives on in the Caesar household.

Bishop Caesar Sr, Geraldine, my dad and other family members were instrumental in nurturing this young man to become a force to reckon with. One of my prayers was that Bishop Caesar Sr. would have a grandson to carry on the ministry. I asked God to honor us with a son whom he could hold in his arms and bless before he closed his eyes in death. God answered my prayer and He was able to hold and bless his only grandson - Hallelujah!

Today, because of the influences of his parents, his family and so many other individuals in his life (too many to list in this addendum- God is keeping a record), we have an emerging spiritual giant in the making : Roderick Richardson Caesar III.

"God never said the journey would be easy,
but He did say that the arrival would be worthwhile."
-Max Lucado-

INTRODUCTION

When I reminisce on the birth of my son, I rejoice in the young man who he has come to be. Because my wife, Beverly had endured two miscarriages, I certainly did not want to see her get pregnant again and suffer another ordeal. I was satisfied with our two lovely daughters and resigned myself to the thought that a son was not in the plan for me. However, when we found ourselves again with child, after the doctor advised against it, I honestly must state that all I really wanted was a healthy baby and for Bev to be okay. Needless to say, God in His divine providence blessed us with a son, and today I am indeed honored.

Ministry is a wonderful medium through which we can serve the Lord and His people. I do not take that responsibility lightly. About 15 years ago I sensed the need to begin looking for someone to succeed me in ministry and I had two capable candidates in mind. God orchestrated their life events so much so that each of them relocated and started their own ministries. By this time it had become apparent to his mother and me that Rod III had spiritually matured and answered the call of God on his life. I sought the Lord concerning His timing. I sat with my son, we prayed and cried and then we set the wheels in motion. I did not want to thrust him into ministry without preparation and validation from the people. So, the timetable was set, that in ten years, from that initial conversation, we would transition the leadership of Bethel into his hands.

It is evident that God's hand is on this young man's life. At the age of 30, he's coming into his own, and is cautiously and prayerfully charting a viable course for Bethel and for the future. He has my full support, my unwavering commitment, my continual prayer and I can rejoice in saying, "I'm overjoyed that he is my pastor."

Our founder (my dad) taught me well. He set the bar high and in wisdom positioned me to take the helm in Bethel when he was still strong, healthy and in his right mind. He was able to watch me shepherd the people whom he pastored for over 40 years.

Bethel Gospel Tabernacle is a historical church right in the heart of South East Queens and has been faithfully serving this community and it's constituents for 87 years. I can boast with godly pride that the pastoral legacy has been passed on to the third generation - what a privilege. Looking at my son walk into his divine destiny brings tears to my eyes. I want him to succeed. I want him to do better than I did. I want him to be a better preacher, teacher and expositor of the Word than I was. He must exceed me in every way, if not, I have failed in training and preparing him.

Leaders who feel that the church cannot function without them are heading in a path of self destruction. God builds His church. We are simply under-shepherds fulfilling God's mandate to lead His people. When leaders feel that they are tied to their pulpit and cannot take a vacation or travel for any length of time because they would come back to a divided church, they have built an **empire** and forsaken the biblical principles of building God's **kingdom**. They have become the head of the church and not Christ.

Again, I thank God for my father's good counsel and godly example. I remember when he passed the baton to me and some members would try to call him "pastor" or would bring a pastoral question to him, he would answer in his strong, stately voice, "I'm no longer your pastor" or he'd simply say, "don't ask me, ask your pastor." He validated me before the people and I am doing the very same thing for my successor.

He's married to a lovely, godly woman, Stefanie. He has a three-year-old daughter, Selah and a three-month-old son, Rod IV. Who knows where God will take this? But of one thing I'm certain - I'm glad to be alive to watch Him unfold another generation of leadership before my very eyes.

Bishop Roderick R. Caesar
International Bishop of BGTFI
Æ

> "When something is important enough,
> you do it even if the odds are not in your favor."
> - John Burroughs-

S.H.O.U.T.

Three decades later	- God's miracle thrives
Three decades later	- God's handiwork survives
Three decades later	- the Caesar family grows
Three decades later	- the community explodes
Three decades later	- Satan remains defeated
Three decades later	- God's glory has not retreated
Three decades later	- the congregation expands in faith
Three decades later	- the millennials take their places
Three decades later	- the foundation's strength races
Three decades later	- the exhorting of the Word teaches
Three decades later	- the preaching of the Word reaches
Three decades later	- the pastoral mantle is passed
Three decades later	- his dad released the torch
Three decades later	- the lot has been cast
Three decades later	- Roderick Caesar, III is the senior pastor!

Stopping and reminiscing about how good God is to me, I cannot help but simply list some of His attributes:

- Everlasting Father - A Heavenly Father who loves us unconditionally.

- Prince of Peace - He keeps us in Perfect Peace if our minds stay focused on Him.

- Almighty God - All mighty, omnipotent, omniscient and omnipresent!

- The I Am that I Am - He is all that and more. Whatever you need Him to be, He is.

- Wonderful Counselor - His advice is seasoned with grace and wisdom.

- Strong Tower - He's our refuge, protection, guidance and peace.

- Name Above all Names - No one can compare to Him and all shall bow to our God.

- Mighty Deliverer - He delivers us from snares, depression; from EVERYTHING!

- Savior. Keeper. Deliverer and Friend - Let's just REPEAT that….. over and over.

- Miracle Worker - We've all experienced His miraculous power in our lives.

- Promise Keeper - NEVER breaks His promise. They are yes and amen.

- Way Maker - He covers our backs and makes a way when there was no way.

I could go on and on with these accolades. He continues to shower His amazing blessings on my life. When I think of His goodness and all He has done for me not only do I sing His praises, but I shout triumphantly with a loud voice. I shout at home, I shout in my car and I shout in the sanctuary. **S.H.O.U.T.** Here's what I do, I:

S	Sing
H	Hallelujah
O	Outrageously
U	Unapologetically *and*
T	Triumphantly

Shout, sing and dance in expectation of your blessing. Sing in anticipation. Sing even though the report may be negative. Joy is coming. The night is soon to end and you will birth forth joy that will come from deep inside your soul. That's what I had to do as I patiently awaited my promise.

Have you ever felt undeserving of His goodness and blessings on your life? **Have you ever wondered** why this Eternal Creator would pour out His love on your life? **Have you ever stopped** to ponder what His purposes are for your life? **Have you ever wished** you could be uninhibited enough to SHOUT out your love to God and not feel embarrassed? Well, what is stopping you? Shout now!

Shout in your shower!
Shout while vacuuming!
Shout in your car!
Shout in the laundromat!
Shout when you wake up in the mornings!
Shout when you get an increase or promotion!
Shout just because you have a job!
Shout in expectation of your miracle!
Shout in anticipation and expectation!
Shout! Shout! And shout again!

Sing **H**allelujah **O**utrageously **U**napologetically and **T**riumphantly!

As I write this addendum, triumphantly thanking God for affording me, my husband, our families, our girls, our church and our communities to witness these 30 years, I cannot help but SHOUT for joy! I consciously and deliberately decide to claim what's mine.

I remember preaching a message that encouraged me to SHOUT and to claim my joy in advance.

Psalm 30: 5 says, *"...in His favor is life: weeping may endure for a night, but joy comes in the morning."* Verse 11 states, *"Thou hast turned for me my mourning into dancing: thou hast put off my sackcloth and girded me with gladness."*

The Psalms is the book of *praises and hymns and spiritual songs.* In the Greek, psalms speaks of a harp or other stringed instrument.

The Psalms were written for singing and public worship in the temple. It wasn't only poems, but lyrics for music. It was written in the language of the human spirit: emotional, dramatic and expressive.

What is weeping? It's simply crying, lamenting, bawling or wailing. As you read through this book or if you read *Experiencing the 25th Hour* you will see that weeping was a common response of mine.

Why do we weep? It's a natural emotional expression. It's a way to mourn the death of a loved one, or even a national disaster such as September 11th. Circumstances of life may cause us to cry or to weep. Hurts, pain, sickness, disappointments, etc. can bring us to an emotional place where weeping gives us relief. Even our savior Jesus, wept.

Keep in mind the text says that it *may endure* for a night. What does this mean? *It simply means a time period was allotted.* It may *continue* for a night; it may *last* for a night or it may *go on* for a night. But one thing is certain, weeping is not permanent - It does not last forever!

According to the Bible when does weeping take place? Literally night is simply a period of time: when the sun sets; when the day is over. Figuratively, the Greek word for night, *laylah*, speaks of a season, it speaks of adversity, a time of distress, death - a time when life's day is over. It speaks of despondency, disappointment, anxiety, What are some of the results? Mood shifts that affect our very countenance, behavior and outlook. It affects our demeanor, our faith.

Some people's nights lasted for days, months and even years. In scripture we have an example of Israel's night with Goliath that lasted 40 days of "nights." Night goes hand in hand with weeping. Weeping is a by-product of your nights...but I declare that your joy is coming so SHOUT!

What is joy? Before I answer that question, joy comes with a price tag! Joy comes with some conditions. Some things you must do to receive this joy. You have to want to be free. So, what is joy? It's a delight of the mind. A response of the mind. It's a deliberate action. The Hebrew word for joy is *gil* which means to leap or spin around with pleasure; to be bright, to shine, to be glad, to spring forth, to be excited, to go in a circle, jubilant shouting. You see, joy rises above circumstances and focuses on the very character of God - Claim this joy now.

How do you get your joy?

Begin with praise and adoration, *"I will extol thee oh Lord."* Stop and remember what He did for you in the past. Sing the song, "I get joy when I thank about what He's done for me."

What should we do now? Sing, shout and give thanks.

- Ask God to give you a song. A song in the night. A song when you are lonely, depressed, heartbroken, heavy, broke, hurt, disappointed, grieving, etc.

- Make up your own song. You are His chosen generation.

- Stop and remember His Word: Joy comes in the morning.

- Your morning can happen at midnight like Paul and Silas in Acts 16.

- Your morning can come in the afternoon through a raise on your job.

- Your morning comes when you accept God at His Word.

- Morning is an understanding of what He is saying to you and your acting upon that Word. II Corinthians 7: *"...you may be troubled on every side but you are not distressed; you may be perplexed but you are not in despair; you may be persecuted but you are not forsaken; you may be cast down but you are not destroyed."* I am sure you are shouting right about now!

Verse 11 of Psalm 30 tells me that He - The Lord - has turned for me my mourning into dancing, so, act on the Word! Your morning is here. Your joy comes in the morning. Your joy is now as you accept His word. He has put dancing in your feet so bless His Name! Even if for whatever reason you may not be able to move your feet, then lift your hands - just move the best way you can. God understands.

Let these scriptures from the Psalms encourage you:

Psalm 8: Oh Lord how excellent is Thy name in all the earth.
(Your morning is now.)

Psalm 20: Some trust in chariots some trust in horses, but I will...
(Let the joy begin.)

Psalm 27: The Lord is my light and...whom shall I fear?
(Take hold of your joy.)

Psalm 32: Thou art my hiding place, Thou shalt preserve me from trouble, Thou shalt compass me about with songs of deliverance.
(Dance before the Lord.)

Psalm 34: Many are the afflictions of the righteous, but the Lord delivers us...
(SHOUT!)

Psalm 42: Why art thou so cast down, oh my soul? ....Hope in GOD for I shall yet praise Him who is the lifter of my countenance, and *who is MY GOD.*
(Praise Him)

Psalm 46: God is our refuge and strength... The Lord of Hosts is with us.
(Hallelujah!)

> "In almost everything that touches our everyday life on earth,
> God is pleased when we are pleased. He wills that we be as free
> as birds to soar and sing our maker's praise without anxiety."
> - A.W. Trozer -

L.I.F.E.

What Satan meant for evil God turned around for good! When Satan thought he had the last word God came through with the first word: **L.I.F.E.**

L	Living
I	Intentionally
F	Faithful
E	Everyday

Each time I look at our son's L.I.F.E. - Roderick Richardson Caesar III, standing at the sacred desk in Bethel Gospel Tabernacle, as my pastor, and faithfully delivering the words of truth, with intention, my heart swells. The godly pride that I feel is indescribable.

Tears well up in my eyes, in my heart and in my spirit. **Tears of joy** - unspeakable joy. Sustained happiness and jubilation flow through my veins and reach to my beating heart. **Tears of thanksgiving** - thankfulness that overflows into a wealth of uncontrollable tears. **Tears of Triumph** - victories over the enemy's plans as I took back what he tried to steal from me. **Tears of a promise fulfilled** - "for this child I prayed." Like Hannah, I honored my vow and gave him back to God.

Years of an amazing journey living before my very eyes. A journey that began 30 years - three decades - 10,957.27 days ago. L.I.F.E. A journey that looked impossible. L.I.F.E. Months that seemed hopelessly grim with endlessly long days! L.I.F.E.

So when did this life begin? June 3, 1989. He was three months early weighing one pound nine ounces. The nurses called him "A 24 weeker." All the odds were stacked up against him. His outcome was far from encouraging. Doctors gave us no hope; they told us he would die in 24 hours because his birth-weight was so low.

At 24 weeks most babies don't make it, especially boys, and if they do live, they become a burden to the parents and to society! As a matter of fact before he was born, my doctor instructed me not to get pregnant again after having two previous miscarriages. Upon his birth, his adamant response was sarcastic as he smirked and said, "See, I told you not to get pregnant again, but you had to go and try for the boy. Well he's here, but he'll die in 24 hours!" I could not allow his negative words to get into my spirit, so as he was speaking I began rehearsing the Word of God.

*"No weapons FORMED against me will prosper." **Isaiah 54:17***

*"God has not given me the spirit of fear, but of love, power and a SOUND MIND." **II Timothy 1:7***

*"The Lord is my light and my salvation, whom shall I fear? The Lord is the STRENGTH OF MY LIFE of whom shall I be afraid?" **Psalm 27:1***

"1 will bless the Lord AT ALL TIMES, His praise shall CONTIN-UALLY be in my mouth." *Psalm 34:1*

*"Fear thou not for I AM WITH YOU. Be not dismayed for I am your God; I will strengthen you, yes, I will help you, yes I will uphold you, with the right hand of my righteousness." **Isaiah 41:10***

I sang, I praised, I worshipped and I rejoiced. I was not going to allow the negativity of the doctor to cause me to become disenchanted or depressed - no way was I allowing that to attach to my spirit. I needed to encourage myself like David did in the Psalms. I needed to triumphantly hold on to His promises and not look back!

When I look at him standing behind the podium and preaching with such fervor, my mind goes back to the first time I saw his tiny body in the isolette - (*a brand of incubator for premature or other new born infants providing controlled temperatures, humidity and oxygen levels and having armholes through which the infant can be reached with minimum disturbance to the controlled environment*).

The verdict looked bleak. The outcome looked like defeat. The hope I had while I was carrying him was waning. What my eyes saw defied logic and reasoning. What my eyes saw caused disappointment to overtake my emotions. What my eyes saw was not the vision I anticipated in motion.

I approached the isolette with caution, trepidation, and fear! Fear? Yes! What I saw was so unbelievable that the thought of death was more powerful than the thought of LIFE! I was afraid to even put my hand through the opening of the isolette to touch his transparent, shriveled, scale-like flesh. I thought that if I touched him he would fall apart in my hand. I thought that if I touched him I would transfer germs into his delicate body. Although my hands were washed, nonetheless my fear of transferring anything that could cause his demise controlled my thinking.

I took off my wedding ring, and carefully and gingerly placed it over his hand with pin-like fingers and cautiously slid it up his pencil-like arm over his elbow and up to his armpit!! Even though, I thought that I was a strong woman of God and full of faith, I couldn't stop the river of tears flowing down my face and soaking my cheeks.

Seeing him in that isolette offered absolutely no hope. What I held onto was the promise that God had given to me while I was carrying him for the short period of time. The hope I held onto was the fact that I prayed and asked the Lord to bless my womb with a son. I had no choice but to hold on - unwaveringly - to the promise of the Living God. This was an answer to prayer. Of course the answer did not come the way I expected or anticipated it. But the journey was necessary.

...the journey was necessary for our church families.

...the journey was necessary for our immediate family.

...the journey was necessary for our extended families.

...the journey was even necessary for our radio audience who prayed us through - who prayed with us believing that God would give us the desires of our hearts.

So, three decades later - 30 years - we are experiencing the miracle for which we prayed! The miracle is still alive and thriving - all praises to our everlasting father, the prince of peace, our miracle working God! A precious LIFE was given to us!

When I look at that young man standing in front of the congregation, or conducting a business meeting, or counseling a couple or talking with a parent concerning their child or children, I look on in amazement at what God did.

It's not about me, it's not about my husband - it's all about our powerful supernatural God who had the vision and knew what our son would become.

L.I.F.E.

"God's work done in God's ways will never lack God's supplies."
- Hudson Taylor -

THE PROMISE KEPT

Penning this addendum to my first book, *Experiencing the 25th Hour*, I write with a feeling of appreciation and amazement of this wonderful God I serve. He honored my prayers and continues to give us the responsibility to wisely and carefully raise our son, this miracle whom He gave to our family and to the church. Because God is a promise keeper I encourage you to hold on to the promises that He made to you and always remember to honor the blessing and not take it for granted. If God can trust you with one miracle, look out for others to come.

I realized during these thirty years that I had to commit his ways to the Lord. When he turned 18, it hit me squarely in the face that he was now a young man with voting privileges, taller than his mother, having a drivers permit, forging friendships and making his own decisions. WOW! Where did the time go? It dawned on me that, as parents we took him as far as we could. No, no we weren't leaving him alone...he was now riding on our prayers, love and support. Two things I still LOVE about him - his tender kisses and his love declarations! I knew his wife and children would never lack those two elements: (a) kisses (b) "I Love You" declarations. I must admit that he learned those attributes from his dad.

As I watched this young man grow from boyhood into manhood and become an amazing preacher and teacher my heart is saturated with emotional gratitude.

When I think about the fact that the doctor said he wouldn't talk until the age of seven because of the tracheotomy - I lift my hands and shout "hallelujah!"

When I reflect on the other diagnoses such as bleeds on the brain, sight problems or cerebral palsy and I look at him and see that he's one hundred percent normal, my praises become radical and I... S.H.O.U.T!

As I function in the marketplace and see other parents with children who are physically disabled I thank God for his blessings on Rod III. When other children have to be transported in wheelchairs or have to travel with medical assistance and oxygen, I lift my hands in thanksgiving to God that the journey he brought us on, or I should say brought us through, is one of total triumph. I silently offer a prayer for these children, their caregivers and their families.

No child is a mistake and each family's journey is unique and special. God equips each of us for the journeys He has ordered us to take. Remember our steps are carefully ordered by the Lord, so walk cautiously. Our God is a Promise Keeper.

As I reflect on my life and my journey, I've come to realize that my life was "set up" by the Almighty God. As I studied His Word and began to preach at conferences, especially to women, I want to share with you one of the narratives I studied. I'm sure this will encourage you.

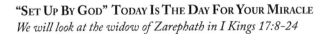

"Set Up By God" Today Is The Day For Your Miracle
We will look at the widow of Zarephath in I Kings 17:8-24

The Day In The Life Of A Widow: An ordinary, unpredictable day, and

God supernaturally turned it around for His glory to give her many more glorious days. He can do the very same for you. As often as you can, begin your day with thanksgiving and expectations. We serve a God who enjoys blessing His people.

BACKGROUND/HISTORY: She was living during the time when Israel was divided into two kingdoms: Northern: Israel and Southern: Judah. Israel was also backslidden with an idolatrous King of the Northern Kingdom who was married to a Baal worshipper - Jezebel from Zion - a Zionian.

However, God always had someone on hand to be His spokesperson to His rebellious children. Elijah the prophet was assigned for this time period to be the voice of God.

He declared a famine on the word of the Lord to the idolatrous King Ahab.

HER LIFE: *(Think about yours and where you are today.)* **God saw her in His providence.** The Latin word for providence is *providentia. Pro* means "before" or "ahead of time"; *videntia* is from *videre,* meaning "to see" from which we get our word video. Put them together and we have "Seeing ahead of time."

I'm encouraged every time I read Romans 11:33, *"Oh the depth of the riches both of the wisdom and depth of God! How unsearchable are His judgments and unfathomable His ways."* His ways are not our ways and His thoughts are not our thoughts. Isaiah 55:9, *"My thoughts are higher than your thoughts"* declares the Almighty God.

Yes, I am talking about our invincible, all knowing, invisible, all wise, eternal, immutable, loving, omnipotent, omniscience, omnipresent, Jehovah Jireh, Jehovah Rapha, Jehovah Shalom, Jehovah Nissi, Jehovah Saboath, Elohim....THAT GOD! He's about to set you up for a miracle. Are you ready? Your breakthrough is closer than you think.

He's already in your future, so He's got your back covered. He only wants the very best for you and your family.

This woman was a foreigner: She was from Zion: Jezebel's home town! She was unknown to us, but God handpicked her for a miracle during a most difficult time - famine. God looks beyond culture, religion, job status, marital status, education, age and gender. He looks inward, while man looks outward. He sees you praying. He hears your heart's cries. He sees your sleepless nights. He hears your groaning and He's moved with compassion.

He knew that her husband died and left her with a son - she was single, a single parent, a widow. It doesn't matter if you are divorced, separated, married or single - God is concerned about you! He sees your hopelessness. He sees your hunger - where is your next meal coming from? He sees your fears and concerns for your family. Remember, if He was mindful of a foreigner how much more care would He give to one of His children?

This woman was near death due to hunger, thirst and lack of strength. How was she feeling? What was going through her mind? Perhaps she felt hopeless, despair, suicidal, felt like taking matters into own hands. The Bible says that when the prophet saw her she was "bent over picking up sticks." Maybe that's where you are spiritually trying to pick up the pieces of your life, but with no faith for victory. You feel as if you are in a pit or headed to the gallows of pain, illness, grief, low self esteem, fractured relationships and financial catastrophe. But hold on - God is setting you up for a miracle! Maybe He made you a promise ten years ago - well, as we've often heard it said, "get ready, get ready, get ready!"

God prepared her. God was working behind the scenes. She knew nothing about what was about to unfold in her life. God touched her heart, attitude and spirit. God sees deep into the recesses of our hearts and sees the true person. He gives hope in place of hopelessness.

HER MIRACLES *(Not only one but two.)* : Miracles happen because of trust and unwavering faith. Although the prophet was a stranger to her and somewhat demanding - telling her to fetch him some water and by the way bring me something to eat while you are at it. Well, the nerve! Some of us would have told him where to go with that attitude!

But you see, because God prepared her spirit, she obeyed his request. She had given up on life and was going to cook her last meal for herself and her son. There wasn't even enough for the two of them. All she had was a handful of meal in the barrel and she was using the last little bit of oil in the cruse - in essence both were empty! Her obedience saved her life, her son's life and blessed the man of God.

Is your life empty? God can fill it to overflowing. Elijah gave her simple instructions that hinged on faith. He told her not to worry about a thing, but to fix him something to eat - first - before she took care of herself she was to bless him first! Wow! How would you have responded?

- God says spend one hour with me, first - *then* watch me bless you.
- God says pay your tithes, first - *then* watch me provide for you.
- God says make the sacrifice and go to Bible Study, first - *then* watch me give you the increase on your job.
- God says call that ailing person, first - *then* watch me heal *your* body.

Obedience is better than sacrifice. As you obey the promises, miracles and breakthroughs will happen in your life - Praise the Lord!

Don't try to fill the barrels in your life. Don't try to fill the emptiness in your lives with your own ingenuities or creativities. This woman obeyed the man of God, and not only did she have enough to feed her son, the prophet, and her household, but more than enough to see her through the famine!! Let God fill your empty barrel. Bring it to him empty! If you fill it with any thing fill it with PRAISE! Here's what God will do with your praise: He will keep the supplies flowing; He will use you to bless someone else; He will continue to perform miracles in your life. Her son died and he miraculously brought him back to life. We still serve a miracle working God!

You will begin to declare truths and praises in your home, on your job, with your families as we read in verse 24, she declared *"...now I know that truly you are a man of God."* This foreigner gained so much from this amazing man of God. If she took it upon herself to learn who he was and recognized the God in him, how much more do we need to learn from God and recognize who He really is?

YOUR SET UP: Realize that where you are in life today is not just for your own good. Where does God have you today? At home, in church, in ministry, on your job, in your community, etc. It is not an accident. God allows things to happen in your life for your good and the good of others. Satan cannot touch you without God's permission. If God released Satan to attack, oppress or distract you, keep in mind that it's for your good and for His glory.

Hold on! Be encouraged! God is not finished with you and your family. He wants to shine forth through you. He wants you to be a blessing to others. Because He's in control of time, we need to be sensitive to His divine direction. As you keep your spiritual ear to His Word and through prayer, I guarantee you that blessings and miracles await you. Promises will be fulfilled in *His* timing! Sometimes God says wait - but in the waiting - praise Him!

THE PROMISE KEPT

"If you can't fly, then run. If you can't run then walk.
If you can't walk then crawl, but whatever you do,
you have to keep moving forward."
- Martin Luther King, Jr. -

PREPAREDNESS

The Bible tells us in Psalm 127, *"Children are a heritage of the Lord: and the fruit of the womb is His reward."* We also read in Proverbs 22 verse 6 that we are to train up our children in the way they should go, so that when they are old they will not depart from it - "it" being the truth of God's Word. Ephesians 6:1 encourages children to obey their parents, in the Lord for this is right. Honor mother and father so that their days may be long on this land.

Parents, we have an obligation to take *good* care of the heritage God entrusted us with. He knew before the foundations of this world that He would bless our womb with the children who we now hold in our arms or who are now standing before us. This responsibility is awesome and can be filled with hope, promise and blessings. It is our duty to train them in the way they should go. They don't know the way - they are looking to us for guidance! No, it is not easy, but with the Lord guiding us and leading the way, we will, by His help lead them to the paths of righteousness.

If for any reason they did not turn out the way you expected, know this one thing - you did your best. You are not a failure! Don't blame yourself for their mistakes. You took them, by the grace and direction of the Holy Spirit as far as you could. If in their adult lives - 18 and older - the choices and decisions they made; on their own, with their own free will; are now having a negative impact on them - just pray. This may sound cliché, but mark my words - prayer works! You have a great weapon in prayer. *"The effectual fervent prayer of the righteous man (person) avails much"* - James 5:16. In the Greek, *effectual* and *fervent* are translated to mean "energy." This conveys the idea of energizing, similarly to the electrical current that brings energy to a circuit. So, this means that your prayer has to be passionate, heartfelt, heated, and persistent. Don't give up because you don't see any immediate change. Hold on, it's coming!

One of the many delightful things that happened in my life or I should say with our son Rod was when we homeschooled him from first grade through the 12th grade. Beth was being homeschooled at the same time from as early as preschool. The curriculum, Abeka, came from a Christian Academy in Florida. It offered a video program with teachers in a classroom setting. Rod and Beth were referred to as "students at home." They had the opportunity to have interaction and participation with the teachers and the video students.

To be successful, Rod and Beth had to be trusted to do the work. I had to be consistent in pushing them not to become distracted or lazy, which was my determined intention - keeping them focused - phew! Needless to say, often times I had to reprimand them for goofing off. Because they were educated at home they did not have to dress to leave the house each day. If you are thinking of homeschooling, here's a behind the scene glimpse of their daily schedule:

Rise & shine (7:30am)
Shower and get dressed
Breakfast and devotions
Video Lessons: part one
Lunch and free time
Video Lessons: part two
Extra-curricular activities
(outdoors - which included Spanish classes)
Dinner
Homework and free time
Bedtime

Depending on our night time endeavors, sometimes I allowed them to sleep late the next day - maybe until 10am.

The flexibility of homeschooling could become a problem if I did not stay focused. I had to keep in mind that one day they would matriculate into the regular school system and needed to have a semblance of order. Sure their days were regimented to a certain degree, but I also allowed for some level of freedom that regular schools did not allow.

As an African American family we were in the minority where home schooling was concerned. My husband and I had to find other homeschooling families outside of our community to create an interactive environment for Rod and Beth. Once we found those families we were able to collaborate on educational trips to the museums, zoos, parks and other social interactive events.

Additionally, what they learned from their father on an ongoing basis - social studies, science, history and English literature - did not come from text books, but from a wealth of experiential knowledge.

I knew it was our responsibility as parents to expose them to the world through the lenses of different experiences. I did not wait for the opportunity to arise, I created the opportunities. I did not want them to become "social misfits" as I was often told they would become!

We did not homeschool arbitrarily or on a whim. We prayed and sought direction from the Holy Spirit and decided this was the best course for our two younger children. NY State had expectations that we had to follow. Guidelines that had to be closely adhered to: IHIP: Individualized Home Instruction Plan. Once approved and included in their system I had to send in a written report to my district office quarterly to ensure that Rod and Beth were fulfilling the hourly requirements. This was demanding and time consuming. I had to keep accurate records of hourly attendance, their tests and exams. Knowing that

God gave me the wherewithal to teach them was another God in-spired moment. Couldn't have done it without His grace and mercy! It wasn't an easy task homeschooling Rod from first grade through the 12th grade at all - to say the least! It was our intention for Rod to matriculate into a public High School, but we missed the 9th grade application window. We thought he could matriculate into the 10th grade, but that was not the NY system's process; hence, it was to our advantage to push him through at home. It would have set him back one year. We learned from this experience, so Elizabeth matriculated into the public school system in the 9th grade.

When it was time for them to take their NY State Citywide Exams, I turned to Bob Jones University which offered tests that were ap-proved by NY State. I needed to find someone to administer the test - a tester - a certified teacher who had to complete an application to qualify for testing. I could not conduct the exams! As a school prin-cipal, a family friend, Renee Dedmon *(Crump - at the time)*, not only graciously accepted my request but she filled that position to a tee. Not once did she complain or offer any resistance. She graciously and professionally rose to the occasion to help us as a family. The exams were sent to her home address. She had to make the time to admin-ister the tests to Rod and Beth in her home. Not once did she offer any excuses! After the tests were completed she mailed them back to Bob Jones University where they were graded, and they in turn sent the results to me! She was honest, forthright and faithful in this task. I'm sure she did not realize that she was indirectly pouring into the life of her future pastor. What a wonderful blessing.

Sometimes we are strategically put into a place to assist, aid, or help others without the apparent blessing staring us in the face. Some-times the results outweigh the sacrifices. Keep in mind that God rewards faithfulness. I'm sure Renee is reaping the benefits of her kindness that will one day showcase in eternity.

Challenging moments surfaced during the homeschooling days. I sometimes thought about giving up and putting them through the regular school system but God kept me going. My husband and I realized how important it was to give them a solid Christian foundation right at home during the process. So, although the task was challenging and sometimes frustrating we pushed through.

For cultural assimilation and social interaction we enrolled them in gymnastics, tennis, basketball and swimming at the YMCA for weekly activities. As pastor's children we saw the importance of music in their lives; hence, musical training and voice lessons were integrated into their weekly activities. They both had piano lessons and later on Beth learned to play the bassoon. It can never be said of Rod and Beth that they were socially disadvantaged or maladjusted!

As your children are obedient and respectful to both parents, Ephesians 6 tells us that they will live long lives. Claim this for your children.

*"The secret of success in life is for a man to be
ready for his opportunity when it comes."*
- Benjamin Disraeli -

KNOWING
THE WORD

The importance of learning the Word of God in their young lives was paramount to their spiritual development. Sunday School and Junior Church *(now Kids4Christ)* assisted in shaping their spiritual acumen and understanding of the Word. Rod was constantly asking questions about the Bible and often times I had to refer him to his dad. Not because I couldn't supply him with the answers, but I wanted him to learn at the feet of his father.

Sunday School and Junior church prepared Rod for what he's doing today. The Bible became, not just a book of stories, but a book of life lessons. As a youngster he wanted to understand those lessons and apply them to his life. He amazed me, like Samuel, of his inquisitiveness and interest in the Word. He loved Sunday School and as the children got older and became their own chauffeurs, he pressed Naomi to get him to church on time! He never wanted to be late.

During Christmas and Easter celebrations, the Sunday School and Junior Church Departments would host programs for Bethel showcasing all the children. It was great seeing Rod and Beth recite seasonal poems, sing in the choir, act in the plays and dramatize the Word of God. As they got older, because of their musical training they were given lead roles in many of the dramatic musicals hosted by Bethel's Fine Arts Ministry.

My prayer is that parents will realize the importance of pouring God's Word into their children at a young age. Parents are the guardians of their children's lives. Kids should not dictate to their parents whether or not they want to go to Sunday School or to a program tailored for their comprehension. The benefits outweigh the negatives. They are being prepared for life - life in general. Sunday school or any similar program teaches the children self control, respect, sharing, and even affords them the opportunity for "public speaking."

Because the Word of God is taught to them in their youth, it is hoped that when they get older it will sustain them. I am observing that some of the millennials who went to Sunday school and children's church with Rod are now in ministry at Bethel serving in leadership roles. What an awesome blessing.

Pouring the Word of God into children whose minds are like sponges is an amazing opportunity for Christian educators to take advantage of such a wonderful audience. These children have a divine connection.

━━━ ◈ ◈ ━━━

Romans 11:33-36; 12:1-2 shows us our **divine connection**. Children, youth and young adults must be taught that they are divinely connected to the Almighty God. Verse 36 lets us know that all things are of Him; all things are through Him and it's all about Him. All things are to Him, concerning Him and for Him.

What things am I talking about? Family, children, spouse, job, car, health, clothing, schooling, education, ministry, finance, etc. are of Him and comes through Him.

In chapter 12:1-2: Paul is saying here and I summarize, in my own words: *Because you live, move and operate, I beg you by the compassion of God, that you give Him yourself at the altar as a **living sacrifice**, holy and acceptable which is the least you can offer, for all He's done for you.* **You must lead by example!**

Looking at verse 2, I have three questions for you as you teach the young people in your lives to be a living sacrifice **(1) Will it be** a good sacrifice? **(2) Will it be** a perfect sacrifice? **(3) Will it be** an acceptable sacrifice? How can this be be accomplished?

Two simple things you must do:
1. **Do not conform to this world:** The Greek means: "to conform to the example of another." Do not conform to the example of the world. I Peter 1: 13-15 tells us and I paraphrase: "gird up the loins of your mind. Be sober, not fashioning yourselves according to the former lusts in your ignorance, but be holy as the Lord is holy."
2. **Transformation of your mind:** What better time to have the minds of the children transformed than when they are young? This is why Sunday School and Children's Church are so important. The Greek word *metamorphosis* simply means "by a supernatural change."

Teach them to:
1. **Know their <u>Purpose</u> like Joseph did:** Have them read and study his life. This scripture make for a very interesting and engaging Bible reading. Genesis 37-50
2. **Know how to <u>Persevere</u>:** DON'T GIVE UP as we read in Esther chapter 4 - about Mordechai. This is another narrative that will keep their attention and give them positive life lessons about holding on and trusting God. Although He was silent in this book, yet He was powerful. Invisible in the text but invincible in His actions as:
   - Jehovah Elohim: My Eternal Creator

- Jehovah Adonai: My Master
- Jehovah Shalom: My Peace
- Jehovah Jirah: My Provider
- Jehovah Shamal: His presence is here
- Jehovah Tsidkneew: Our Righteousness
- Jehovah Saboath: Lord of Hosts

3. **Know that <u>Prayer</u> changes things:** Daniel chapter 6 takes us where Daniel was - in the Lion's Den. But he was connected to God because of his prayer life. God did not take him out of the den but kept him there as He shut the mouths of the lions.

4. **Know how to <u>Praise</u> in the midst of the trial:** Paul and Silas praised their way out of a prison cell - Read Acts 16.

You never know who you may be teaching.....a future pastor, doctor, president of the USA , a lawyer or preacher.

"God can use the words of a teenager, the prayer of a senior citizen, or the candid remark of a child to convict you of the need to make changes in your life."
- Henry T. Blackaby -

ANSWERING THE CALL

When graduation time came we wanted him to have the experience of walking across the stage to personally receive his hard earned High School diploma. As a family we packed up and flew to Pensacola Christian Academy in Florida. We watched with excitement the expressions of awe on his face as he would see and meet some of his video teachers in the flesh!

Walking across the stage to receive his High School diploma was not only a momentous occasion for him but for me as well. I reveled in the moment absorbing the feeling of godly pride and gratitude knowing that I had something to do with this grand occasion. I held my head high, stuck out my chest with honor as he shook hands with the academic dean to receive his diploma. For this boy I prayed and God trusted me to enjoy another indescribable experience. The entire Caesar family enjoyed the moment. This goes down in history as one of our best memorable vacations we enjoyed as a family- a true double hitter!

Then of course the next step was getting him into a college. Completing application after application was tedious but necessary. We asked God to lead us to the right college. The outcome was easier than I anticipated. He was accepted into four different colleges straight from homeschool - imagine that! He was offered music scholarships but he had a propensity for history; hence, he felt that's the direction he would go in. However, after one of his music auditions, the director suggested that we take him to an ear nose and throat specialist to ensure that his vocal cords were not compromised. They felt his voice had a raspy tone that could have something to do with his prematurity! Keep in mind that his vocal cords were paralyzed at birth!

We were given a suggested list of specialized doctors in our area to choose from and I contacted one of them and set up the appointment. The doctor's name seemed somewhat familiar but I really paid it no attention. When I arrived at the doctors office, his name began ringing over and over in my mind. Why does his name seem so familiar? I couldn't get the connection until I saw him! He was still handsome, older, but now he had a head filled with gray hairs! He was the surgeon who performed the tracheotomy on Rod when he was two months old! Who would have thought that this very doctor would be examining him 16 years later. In my book *Experiencing the 25th Hour*, he's referred to as Dr. Weeks. He recognized Rod's name and remembered him quite well. What stood out in his memory was that Rod was the third of three Rodericks! He also remembered that we were a close knit family who visited Rod everyday.

Surprisingly the doctor found nodules on his vocal cords! Nothing alarming, but if he were to major in music he would need to have therapy to get rid of the nodules. The doctor informed us that nodules were common in teachers, politicians and preachers and anyone who did a lot of public speaking. He said laughing out loud - forcefully - on a daily basis could cause nodules on the vocal cords. What was the simple remedy? Drinking water regularly and consciously; making the effort not to yell, shout, scream or laugh forcefully would aid in diminishing the nodules although not eradicating them entirely.

However, as he began rethinking his major he answered the call of God on his life and pursued ministry. Here's how he recalls the experience:

I didn't grow up wanting to be a pastor. In fact my desire was to be involved in anything but ministry. Part of the reason is that I wanted to be my own person, blaze my own trail and thought that if I ended up being in the same profession as my father and grandfather I would somehow lose who I was. I had plans for my life, and none of them involved preaching and shepherding people.

That all changed one summer night at my church's summer camp, Camp Joharie. That was over 10 years ago and I remember as if it were yesterday. We had a church service and our leaders told us to pray about our purpose and what God wanted for us. So, with some hesitation, I asked God to speak to me about what I was supposed to do with my life.

Immediately, I saw a photograph hanging on a wall. It was taken when I was around 3 years old, and there I was sitting with my father, and grandfather - three generations. With that picture I heard the phrase "you're next stop running." God showed up that night in the service and the Holy Spirit began to move. People were praying for individuals and three different people came and prayed for me and said - you guessed it- , "you're next stop running." I broke down because I knew I was running from what God had called me to do, and that night I decided to stop running and submit to God's word over my life.

When I got back from camp I spoke with my parents about my experience. Mom was quiet and pensive. Dad seemed moved by my testimony, but said he had to hear from God for himself, he needed clarity - and he did just that. He also needed to be sure this was what the Lord wanted! Several months later, after getting confirmations from the Lord, he reintroduced me to the congregation as their next pastor.

Seemed a little hasty but I assure you because he too was looking for anyone but me. He had other individuals in mind to be the pastor but each individual ended up going in different directions - outside of our church. What we both didn't know was that God was going to call me to the ministry. So once my call was confirmed, to prepare the congregation for when that time would came, he informed them so that they would pray for me as I prepared to walk on the journey toward pastoral ministry.

So that's how this journey came into being. A praying mother, a son with a vision from the LORD and an obedient Father were all in God's plan of getting me where I am right now, and I couldn't be more grateful. 30 years in and this is only the beginning. Praise God.

Walking in the footsteps of his grandfather who founded Bethel, built the ministry with seven branch churches, a credit union, a radio broadcast, a Bible school and a sleep away camp in the Catskills were daunting accomplishments. To top it off, his dad continued the Bethel brand by adding a television ministry, expanding the radio ministry, acquiring new properties, establishing outreaches, and taking the Bible school internationally. His father also interfaced with national and global organizations expanding the scope of BethelGT to an International level. He realized that a lot was expected of him and he did not want to fail. Because of the overwhelming tasks facing him, the anticipation weighed heavily on him since he knew he would be judged by their standards. Thank God he's charting his own course, his own way and today as he stands on the shoulders of two great men, he's looking forward to carving out his own legacy leaving his own set of footprints.

I silently observe him interfacing with people and I am proud to say that teaching him to be a gentleman is paying off. I remember telling him as a young boy to treat his sisters with respect, open the doors for them and to assist them in and out of the car. I would often say when we would get home late in the evenings or at nights, "never allow me or your sisters to be the last ones to enter the house. See that we are safely inside, then secure it."

You know how siblings treat each other and I would often times hear his sisters say to him, "You are our slave, so open the door!"

I reprimanded them and said, "One day he's going to grow up and the tables will turn, so be careful what you say to him."

Of course as children they continued with the teasing. I also told him to value the elderly, to give them honor and treat them with dignity. Watching him interface and interact with his peers and with the elderly puts him head and shoulders above so many others. He genuinely loves people and would take the shirt off his back for the seniors.

"Opportunity doesn't make appointments,
you have to be ready when it arrives."
- Tim Fargo -

CALLED TO LEAD
BY LISA RAY
(Lisa wrote this poem expressly for Pastor Rod)

I've been called to lead you
Now will you pray, you see I answer to God
As He prepares me on what to say
I am committed to live holy and be an example to you all
While it is a part of my history, my legacy,
It is in fact an answered call
Obedience is better than sacrifice
And I choose to serve King Jesus
He paid the price giving His life
So life would be better, yes eternal for us
I was raised right here in Bethel the house of God,
A vision founded by my grandfather Bishop Roderick Senior,

Who planted and taught you well.
So much so many would excel in God,
In fact my dad followed him, as he followed Christ
Bishop Roderick number two for many years he served us too.
Now we are here for all to see the legacy continue…
with Pastor Roderick Caesar III making it three times, how nice
So let's rejoice and continue to pray.
I've been called to lead you and God makes a way.

"Man make history not the other way around.
In periods where there is no leadership, society stands still.
Progress occurs when courageous, skillful leaders seize the
opportunity to change things for the better."
- Harry S. Truman -

HOLD ON!

Has God ever made a promise to you that you're still expecting to see fulfilled? I am certain if you are a born-again believer or a Christian who loves the Lord that He certainly made some promises to you which perhaps you have already seen fulfilled or the fulfillment is on its way. Don't give up, hold on, God will make a way, God has made a way. Our faith is sometimes tested and tried as we wait and hold on! Keep in mind that God has not forgotten to come through with the promise He made to you.

- Promises for your family - Hold on!
- Promises for your health - Hold on!
- Promises for your financial stability - Hold on!
- Promises for your children - Hold on!
- Promises for the salvation of your loved ones - Hold on!
- Promises to prosper your way - Hold on!
- Promises to save your marriage - Hold on!

I'm sure you could add on to this list - promises to keep you in perfect peace as your mind stays on Him. I encourage you to extend your faith to believe that because we serve a God who is true and faithful to His Word - He will deliver, so HOLD ON!

As I reflect on God and His promises to my family from fulfilling the promise that a son would be born into this family to Bishop Caesar

Sr. holding that promise in his hand proves to me that God is true to His word. Although the doctors gave me some negative reports that if I did get pregnant again I would lose the baby. I had no recourse but to hold on to His promise.

Even though I had two beautiful daughters Naomi and Lydia, I wanted a son! I was happy yet anxious about having another child because of my previous miscarriages. I prayed for this boy and asked God to bless my womb one more time. I really wanted the Caesar name to continue through the lineage and the heritage of a male child. Sure my girls were capable to lend oversight to the ministry. Of course they were qualified and gifted. However I wanted the Caesar name to live on. I wanted the legacy to move forward. So I was specific in my request.

Sometimes we are not specific in our prayer requests to God. We are too general or too basic in our appeals to God. The Lord wants us to be specific and poignant in our asking. He tells us to come boldly into the throne room and make our requests known. I asked for a son! Now, we know He's a sovereign God. We know we serve an awesome God and He will make the ultimate decision, but He instructs us to ask. Not any arbitrary request with no specificity or validity. A request that will bring honor to God. A request that will honor your family and, for a lack of a better expression something that "will make God look good."

This addendum is written to encourage you. It's written for you to hold on with faith and trust God that the promises he made will come to fruition.

Sometimes the promise looks like it's never coming or it looks like if it comes it would be defective. God gave me the promise on a night in my church that I'll never forget. So I held on to that memory. I wrote it in my journal. I didn't even share it with my husband. I held my peace. Some promises need to be kept close and personal and that's just what I did. Some people's faith is not on the same level with your faith and unintentionally they may discourage your heart. Therefore you keep the promise in your heart and watch God do the unfolding. So, when I got pregnant I knew I was going to have a son.

I was not surprised after going into the hospital that I would be giving birth to a boy. I did not expect that he would arrive early and with so many medical challenges. My husband was there for the delivery. I was asleep, so when I awakened he was sitting by the bedside.

Our conversations went something like this as I asked, "How is he?"

"How do you know it's a boy?" he replied.

"Trust me, God promised me a son so I know it's a boy," I said with confidence and assurance.

His response to me was that he was not doing well at all and that he was very, very small. The doctors gave us no hope. I was in and out of consciousness because of the anesthesia so I dozed off back to sleep. I was awakened by the doctor in my face. He indicated to me that Rod would not live. He spoke with such confidence that for a moment I was beginning to have doubts. Although he came to me with those negative words I held onto the promise that God had given to me.

A week later I was able to go and see my premature 1lb. 9 oz. son laying in an isolette. For a split second my faith wavered. My heart sunk. How can this promise live? I asked myself. I knew what I had to do. I had to pull up on my faith, pull up on my confidence and pull up on the Word of God. That's what I had to do. I had to remember what God told me and that's just what I did. I had to hold on! Each time that I look at him in that pulpit preaching the word of God, exhorting with power and the anointing my heart becomes overwhelmed with awe at the blessings of God on his life!

As I pen this addendum you will read the word "overwhelmed" several times. I cannot overuse it to express to you, that yes, I was overwhelmed as I watched this boy go from one hospital to another receiving negative reports from one doctor to the next concerning his viability. Hearing the negativism from doctors and nurses alike broke my heart. Not many in the medical field offered us any hope. A few nurses tried to be encouraging but when they presented their medical opinions the outlook was bleak. So what did I do? I had to hold on to the promise! If you hold this book in your hands or if you are reading on a tablet I'm encouraging you to do the same; hold on to the promise that the Living Almighty God gave to you. It's not what you hear or what your eyes see - just know that God is fighting for you.

- *Fighting because He knows* the battle is already won.
- *Fighting because He knows* He loves you dearly and He wants to see the promises fulfilled in your life.
- *Fighting because He knows* you are already looking out in victory.
- *Fighting because He knows* that Satan has lost this battle.
- *Fighting because He wants* to encourage your heart and encourage your spirit.
- *Fighting because He knows* the thoughts that he has for you to prosper you and to give you a great expected end.

Hence we walk by faith not by sight and we believe God because His Word is yea and amen, so just hold on!

"There is no substitute for hard work. Never give up.
Never stop believing. Never stop fighting."
- Hope Hicks -

"Life is about how much you keep fighting;
how much you can suffer and keep moving forward."
- Anderson Silva -

A CLOSE ENCOUNTER OF THE PRAYING KIND

As I previously mentioned, Hannah became a close companion of mine while I was waiting on the Lord to heal my womb and deliver a male child into my arms. Let me share with you how God unfolded this text to me from 1 Samuel.

A CLOSE ENCOUNTER OF THE PRAYING KIND
Do you want this encounter?
I Samuel 1:5

The Bible is filled with examples of close encounters, such as, The Virgin Mary - the Mother of Jesus; the Samaritan woman at the well; the woman with the issue of blood; Martha; Mary Magdalene and the list goes on. But come with me on a journey of a woman who found the secret to HOLDING ON despite all the odds that were stacked up against her.

Let's look at a woman who experienced her encounter through the powerful tool of prayer: We will look at her from 3 positions:

1. Before she prayed.

2. During her prayer.

3. After she prayed.

In I Samuel 1:5 we read, *"But unto Hannah he gave a worthy portion (Elkanah): for he love Hannah: But the LORD had shut up her womb."*

Let's look at the backdrop to this narrative:
Israel was in a backslidden state. Apostasy had become the rule of the day. There was sinning in the tabernacle and rebellion was rampant! Sound familiar?

Hannah was married to a good man who took pride in caring for his family, but there was one issue - he had another wife whose name was Peninnah! He was also a godly man as he ensured that every year he would take his family on the long pilgrimage to Shiloh to sacrifice unto the Lord.

He loved Hannah, but she was unhappy! Why? She was barren, childless, empty, unfulfilled, unaccomplished and incomplete. She wanted a baby to hold in her arms - but God had shut up her womb. No man could undo what GOD had done!

But God's love superseded her husband's. **We have to get to the place where we can see God in our pain and not blame the devil or our loved ones.** This was her own experience, her own personal cross, her own trial, her own test. God chose to SHUT up her womb. The Eternal Creator - Jehovah Elohim - allowed this to happen because he loved her! Sometimes your journey is to grow you up in God and give you divine confidence!

The Hebrew word *cagar* means to close or to imprison. She was in her own private prison. Surrounded by family but in prison; an emotional and mental prison. This word is found 80 times in the O.T. The first reference is found in Genesis 2:21, *"And the Lord God caused a deep sleep to fall upon Adam and he slept: and he took one of his ribs, and* ***closed up*** *the flesh thereof."*

This refers to the **shutting up of something**. But in God's shutting there are no scars, but a smooth operation. There is always a reason for the shutting! God had her in this place for a divine purpose, **and no one** could prevent it from unfolding. In the fullness of His time the curtains will draw back.

Before she prayed, her condition was grievous in two ways:

1. Her adversary (the other wife) provoked her sore as we read in verse 6. Provoked in the Hebrew is *"ka ac"* meaning *to anger*, to cause someone to be grieved, to vex. Her adversary caused her trouble and distress.

2. She also made her fret, which is *"ra am"* in the Hebrew and means *to thunder* or *cause to tremble*. Hannah was not happy at all. Here she was in the same house with the other wife who was pushing out babies regularly. Peninnah taunted her and flaunted in her presence the obvious issue!

She was encouraged by her husband as verse 8 shows. He did his best to show his love to her and even asked her if he wasn't better to her than 10 sons. Yet she continued to fret. She ate but with no enthusiasm because she had no appetite. She ate out of obligation to her husband and because of the feast.

> *"Trouble and perplexity drive us to prayer,*
> *and prayer drives away trouble and perplexity."*
> **- Melancthon -**

During her prayer:
On one specific journey to Shiloh, Hannah decided to find a quiet place in the temple to talk to the Lord. She wanted a close encounter. She left her family and went to the altar and verse 10 reads... *"and she was in bitterness of soul, and prayed unto the Lord, and wept sore."*

We note three conditions of her soul as she cried out to the Lord. I'm sure she was desperate. Some prayers are desperation prayers. Let's look at the following:

1. **She was sorrowful.**
2. **She wept.**
3. **She vowed a vow** in verse 11. She made God a promise. She made an agreement with the Lord of Lords. Remember, all vows were made to God as a promise in expectation of HIS favor (Genesis 28:20) OR in thanksgiving of His blessings - (Psalm 116:12-14). Vows had to be paid to God in the congregation at the tabernacle. Just as Hannah made a vow to God, so did I. I promised Him that if He blessed my womb with a male child I would give him back to God - and I meant it just like Hannah did. The next observation in the text is important.
4. **She was being observed** as we read in verses 13 and 14. Eli, the Priest was in the temple watching her as she prayed and he began reading her lips. People are watching you. Observing your life! Interestingly enough this priest who couldn't keep order in his home, this priest who allowed sin to blatantly take place in the temple missed the mark.
5. **She was misjudged.** He thought she was drunk! Imagine that! The man of God missed it. Have you ever been misunderstood or misjudged? What was your response? You better know God for yourself. Once she explained to him that she wasn't drunk but was crying out to God, things changed for her.
6. **She was blessed by the Priest.** He told her that God heard her cry and that in nine months she was going to give birth to a son. Well, needless to say, she got up, thanked him and went on her way.

"When we pray, it is far more important to pray with a sense of the greatness of God than with a sense of the greatness of the problem.
- Evangeline Blood, a Wycliffe Bible translator -

After she prayed:

Verses 18-20 *"...So the woman went her way, and did eat, and her countenance was no more sad. And they rose up in the morning early, and worshipped before the Lord, and returned, and came to their house and Elkanah knew his wife, Hannah **and the Lord remembered her.** Wherefore it came to pass, when the time came about after Hannah had conceived, that she bare a son and called his name Samuel, because I have asked him of the Lord."*

After Hannah prayed, she ate, she was happy, her countenance changed and she worshipped. Her God who had shut her womb opened it and she conceived. What are you conceiving? what visions are you planning to birth? God opened what He had closed - Hallelujah! And sure enough when Samuel was weaned and became of age she honored her vow and gave him back to God and he became the first prophet in Israel bringing order to a house that was in chaos.

I encourage you to come in close through prayer. Come for a close encounter. Come up close and take a look. Get in His face. God is paying attention. You need the experience you are in! God is in it with you. You will see things through His eyes. Your countenance will change. Your appetite will change. The things you once yearned for will no longer be important. He will give you His desires. His ways are not our ways, but you'll begin to understand His ways. Your focus will change. You will see your adversary differently and even begin praying for your enemy. He's waiting to meet with you. He's longing for that encounter. Go down in history for having an encounter with God.

Leave this legacy for your children, grandchildren, and great grand children to remember you by. Be numbered with the Marys, the Elisabeths, the Marthas and the Hannahs. This encounter could change your future.

"Gratitude bestows reverence, allowing us to encounter everyday epiphanies, those transcendent moments of awe that change forever how we experience life and the world."
- John Milton -

ONE FLESH

Marriage for Rod III was a thought that stayed in the back of my psyche. Of course I wanted him to get married! He needed a strong godly woman who would fit perfectly into the Caesar and Bethel families. That was my constant prayer. I had no preference as to her nationality or church background as long as she would respect and honor him and bless our households with the pitter-patter of little feet. Bishop Jacqueline McCullough preaches at Bethel on a regular basis and over the years she dropped certain nuggets of truth that I repeated and still repeat to my children. I will never forget these two nuggets - God rewards faithfulness and He is already in your future. I repeated those nuggets of truth to my children over and over so much so they believed they came from my head. So, I never pressured Rod about marriage or his dating exploration. I left his decision in the hands of the Lord who certainly was already in his future!

Because he remained private with his courting experiences, I didn't press him in that area. My thought was that God would prepare him for the right woman. We did our best to teach him godly principles that would take him into a healthy relationship. His father took him out on many occasions for their one on one father son talk - I kept my prayerful distance.

The Bible is clear when it tells us that a man who finds a wife finds a good thing. That "good thing" was out there for him to find. I prayed for wisdom, discernment, caution and a sensitivity to the voice of the

Lord. He needed to hear God for himself. He needed to follow his heart and hopefully not become pulled into any subtle distractions. Because God's hand was on his life and I wanted to ensure that his purpose wouldn't be compromised by any of Satan's devices, I stayed in an attitude of warfare prayer.

God's timing is amazing.
His plans never fail.
He works on our prayers while we are sleeping.
God knows what's best for us.

He even knows the college your children should attend. With that being said, we had an idea of the college we thought would be ideal for Rod to attend. It was a Christian college with the curriculum he desired and of course we wanted him to feel fulfilled in his education. His dad did not want his connection with some of these colleges to influence the decision-making in any way whatsoever. However, the minute the attendance dean saw Rod's name they immediately connected it to his father. But God had another college in mind. A college that was outside of his dad's close connection. He was given some financial assistance in all the colleges that accepted him, but Gordon College was the most financially gracious and - the rest is history.

Who knew that this was where he'd meet his wife Stefanie?
Who knew that she would be Indian and Chinese?
Who knew that she'd be beautiful, smart and anointed? GOD DID!!
She was perfect for Rod III.
She was perfect for the Caesar family.
She was perfect for BethelGT.

The meeting of the Caesar and Wong families was planned and we drove to Boston for the encounter. The Chinese culture and heritage we experienced through Stefanie's grandparents - her dad's parents - were educational and memorable. Her Fijian born mom welcomed us with open arms and the family bond was formed immediately!

The wedding plans were made and God gave our families a delightfully enjoyable and memorable celebration as two families forged a united bond. To watch all three of his sisters and his niece, Kayliah fully involved in the bridal party and in the festivities warmed my heart. Stef's niece, Audrey made her debut as the flower girl. As he watched his bride walk down the aisle to meet him is another special moment in my arsenal of precious memories. My son the man. My son the husband, and eventually awaiting him as my son - the minister.

"L.O.V.E. is - Living Our Vows Everyday."
- Beverly Morrison Caesar-

KAIROS MOMENTS

Let me explain this important word that unfolded in his life:

The word *kairos* was an ancient Greek word meaning "opportunity," "season," or "fitting time." Another Greek word for "time" was *chronos*. A sequence of moments was expressed as *chronos*, emphasizing the duration of the time; an appointed time was expressed as *kairos*, with no regard for the length of the time. Thus, *chronos* was more linear and quantitative, and *kairos* was more nonlinear and qualitative.

The Bible uses the word *kairos* and its cognates 86 times in the New Testament (e.g., in Matthew 8:29; Luke 19:44; and Acts 24:25). The word often includes the idea of an opportunity or a suitable time for action to take place. When we "seize the day," we are taking advantage of the *kairos* given to us. *Kairos* is related to the Greek word *kara* ("head"). A *kairos* is a time when things "come to a head," requiring decisive action.

In Jesus' parable of the wheat and the tares, the Lord refers to the coming judgment as a harvest: *"At that time [kairos] I will tell the harvesters: First collect the weeds and tie them in bundles to be burned; then gather the wheat and bring it into my barn"* - Matthew 13:30. By using *kairos* here, Jesus emphasizes the fact that Judgment Day is an appointed time, and at that time will occur certain things appropriate for the day.*

*Information gathered from www.wikipedia.com

When I stop and analyze the rapid pace of Rod's maturing into manhood I stand in amazement. His dad announced to the congregation that he was passing the mantle to Rod when he was just about 18. His father wanted the congregation to be fully involved in the unfolding of the historic transition. He did not want to simply thrust him into the drivers seat without training, molding and preparation.

Those ten years rapidly went by and my son, finished school, obtained his M.Div., was licensed as a minister, then ordained as Rev Roderick Caesar III and finally installed as the senior pastor of Bethel-GT. These god-ordained **kairos moments** in his life are momentous events that serve to shape his divine destiny. The rapidity at which they unfolded made me realize that his legacy was being shaped as he was charting his own course for his life and BethelGT.

> *For this son I prayed.*
> *Overwhelmed.*
> *Blessed.*

He's come a long way. Maturing and growing into the role of preacher, teacher and pastor takes time. I watched him start out taking baby steps and feeling his way around, almost as if in the dark. He had some large shoes to fill- those of his grandfather and his father; sure he intended to learn from them but doing so while walking in his own shoes.

I remember one Sunday morning as I sat and attentively listened to my pastor teach I was filled to overflowing. He was teaching me. I was sitting at his feet and learning how to navigate through life's challenges. He was encouraging me. The tears swelled up again and I became overwhelmed as I watched him walking in his purpose.

He was teaching us that sometimes life's circumstances make us question if God really cares. As people we struggle seeing past the storm. We can't see pass the fact that moving forward is a possibility while believing that His grace is enough. As I listened I remembered having those feelings, wondering if this day that I was experiencing would ever be a reality. What an awesome reality I am privileged to experience - hallelujah!

As he continued with the narrative of Jesus calming the storm, he said, "His disciples were following His instructions to get in the boat and go to the other side. Jesus led them into the storm. Jesus knew what was coming and then He went to sleep! Although He was God, He could only be in one place at one time because he was clothed in human flesh. Storms are usually paired with suffering. There's life on the other side of the suffering. Jesus was not surprised. He wasn't caught off guard. He was in complete and full control. He was at peace. We cannot be separated from His love. A word that speaks out to the chaos: Peace be still as he spoke to the wind and the waves. Be anxious for nothing."

Listening to him preach that sermon I just began thanking God for being in the storm with me when he was in the hospital. Being with me in the emergency room time, and time again, when he developed pneumonia or when his trachea tube popped out of his neck, or when he had a viral infection or his fever was so high they had to keep him overnight. God was with me whispering…peace…peace… peace each and every time! And look at him now Experiencing his 30th year - pastoring!

Three years ago " father" was added to his long lists of rapid growth and achievements - another *kairos* moment. Selah came into the world one cold December while hubby and I were vacationing in Massachusetts. Oh the joy that saturated my heart when I was able to hold Rod's daughter in my arms- what an awe inspiring moment! Just to think that my miracle son was now a dad made my feet weak and my heart flutter with pride. Satan never intended for this to happen but as my son, my pastor taught us one Sunday morning, "...life may throw some difficulties your way, just know that God still works miracles!" And by the publication of this book another miracle will be birthed - our grandson Roderick Richardson Caesar IV, another *kairos* moment and the legacy thrives!

"There are special moments of incredible closeness with God when you discover something new about who He is and about who you are."

- UNKNOWN -

THE LEGACY EXPANDS

When Rod and Stef got pregnant with their second child the excitement in the air was contagious. Everyone shared in the joy of the possibility of another Caesar addition to the family! A boy? Another girl? Well that was up to the Lord, but I was hoping for a boy. Should he be called Rod the fourth keeping within the tradition? Well, that was up to the parents! I hoped that they would keep the legacy in perpetuity, but again, I'm only the grandmother.

During the second trimester of the pregnancy they revealed the gender to us - it was going to be a boy! His birthdate was sometime between March 12th and the 17th of 2019. Well, the only challenge for me and my husband was that we had a previously planned vacation on the Disney Wonder to be with Beth who was a Main Stage Performer on the ship. We were scheduled to be home on March 10th. Knowing babies and their unpredictability of gracing us with their presence was totally in the hands of the Almighty - only time would tell. I was hoping he'd stay in his cocoon until around March 10th.

But on March 5th we were at dinner on the ship - we had crossed through the Panama Canal and were on the open seas for three days, simply relaxing and resting. That evening, Beth joined us for dinner.

Before the first course was even served excitement filled the air as her brother texted her with the great news of our grandson's birth. How could I remain composed? How could I contain my jubilation? How was I supposed to hold back feelings of excitement and awesomeness that were flooding my emotions all at once?! My hubby had tears of joy in his eyes!

We wanted to be there. We wished we were there. They needed me... no, no, they don't need you! You are where you're supposed to be, with Beth - **she** needs you! God knew this day would be and since our steps are ordered by the Lord, then simply rest! And that's just what I did. I prayed, I blessed God and I rested.

They sent us photos of the little guy with proud daddy and his precious mommy! What a blessing for cellphones with FaceTime features. I was just elated that his mom pushed through a long labor to usher into the world a seven pounds two ounces, 21inches healthy baby boy. That night we had an opportunity to chat with them. The legacy lives on.

My mom would have been so proud. I remember her walking around and singing to all the pre-term babies in the neonatal unit in the hospital while Rod III was there:

> *"He's got the whole world, in His hands.*
> *He's got the whole wide world, in His hands.*
> *He's got the whole world, in His hands.*
> *He's got the whole world in His hands.*
>
> *"He's got the little tiny babies, in His hands.*
> *He's got the little tiny babies, in His hands.*
> *He's got the little tiny babies, in His hands.*
> *He's got the whole world in His hands."*

To see her grandson bring forth her great grand son into this world, I'm sure she's beaming from heaven.

And what about his grandfather, the man who said an unconditional yes to God and started this legacy of Caesar priesthood? The baby he held in his arthritic arms and although unable to see his grandson, he embraced the miracle nonetheless. I'm sure he's celebrating in heaven the arrival of his great grand son who will ensure that his name lives on for generations to come. What a blessing that I am included in this rich legacy.

Satan wanted to kill me before I came into the world. Some of you may know my story but I will share a small part of it to encourage you. Read it's entirety in *Experiencing the 25th Hour*. My parents, Hector and Veronica Morrison planned to abort me, but God intervened. At the time they got pregnant with me they were living in a one room house with my two older siblings - kitchen and bathroom were on the outside. They just couldn't afford to have another child, so a relative encouraged them to abort me. Unsaved and seeing that as a practical option they headed for the doctor, but God showed up and shut down Satan's plans. You see, things could have turned out differently! Every year on my birthday, May 12th, I share this miraculous blessing with BethelGT and I S.H.O.U.T. with the voice of triumph.

"The greatest legacy one can pass on to one's children or grandchildren is not money or other material things accumulated in one's life, but rather a legacy of character and faith."
- Billy Graham -

THE PASTOR SPEAKS

EPILOGUE
MORE THAN ENOUGH
Sermon manuscript by Pastor Roderick Caesar, III

JOHN 6:1-15 (ESV)

[1] After this Jesus went away to the other side of the Sea of Galilee, which is the Sea of Tiberias. [2] And a large crowd was following him, because they saw the signs that he was doing on the sick. [3] Jesus went up on the mountain, and there he sat down with his disciples. [4] Now the Passover, the feast of the Jews, was at hand. [5] Lifting up his eyes, then, and seeing that a large crowd was coming toward him, Jesus said to Philip, "Where are we to buy bread, so that these people may eat?" [6] He said this to test him, for he himself knew what he would do. [7] Philip answered him, "Two hundred denarii worth of bread would not be enough for each of them to get a little." [8] One of his disciples, Andrew, Simon Peter's brother, said to him, [9] "There is a boy here who has five barley loaves and two fish, but what are they for so many?" [10] Jesus said, "Have the people sit down." Now there was much grass in the place. So the men sat down, about five thousand in number. [11] Jesus then took the loaves, and when

he had given thanks, he distributed them to those who were seated. So also the fish, as much as they wanted [12] *And when they had eaten their fill, he told his disciples, "Gather up the leftover fragments, that nothing may be lost."* [13] *So they gathered them up and filled twelve baskets with fragments from the five barley loaves left by those who had eaten.* [14] *When the people saw the sign that he had done, they said, "This is indeed the Prophet who is to come into the world!"* [15] *Perceiving then that they were about to come and take him by force to make him king, Jesus withdrew again to the mountain by himself.*

This is a familiar portion of Scripture and the only miracle Jesus performed other then his own Resurrection, that is found in all four Gospels. This lets us know it's somewhat of a big deal.

The objective is to remind some of you and inform others about the majesty of our great God. There are three quick observations I'd like to point out from this text.

1) DON'T MISS THE MOMENT FOR A MIRACLE

The crowd was in need and the disciples didn't realize it, and if they realized it they didn't care enough to try and do something about it. In the other gospels we see that the disciples were trying to send these people away. Elsewhere in Scripture we also see them trying to send away children. In both instances they seemed too preoccupied with the way they thought things should be instead of seeing things with compassion as Christ did.

My prayer is that we don't get so caught up in how we feel or how we see, that we miss the moment for a move of God. Sometimes we are the barrier to our blessing. The thing is, God often wants to work in our lives through our obedience, but are we willing to see things His way and step out in faith?

Think about the fact that they almost missed their moment. How many moments have we missed? How many opportunities for God to move through us and in various situations have we passed by, or pushed away?

That's why it's so important to have the mind of Christ. To see things how God sees things. Jesus once said, *"I don't do anything unless I see the father doing it."* I pray that our prayers become:

> "Lord... I want to see with your eyes...
> I want to hear with your ears...
> I want to speak with your lips...
> I want to feel with your heart...
> I want to be changed from the inside out."

God help us to surrender; God help us not to miss out on divine opportunities for You to have Your way.

2) IN YOUR WEAKNESS GOD IS STRONG
In verse 5, Jesus said to Philip, *"Where are we to buy bread, so that these people may eat?"* In the other Gospels this question is asked to the disciples as well.

Something I've noticed about the LORD is that even though God is all knowing, he's not beneath asking a question or two.

Verse 6 gives us some extra insight, *"He said this to test him, for he himself knew what he would do."*

When God asks us questions, they are for our clarity and not His; for our understanding and not His. See, He is all knowing and outside of time and even though Jesus subjected himself to living inside of time, he was deeply in tune with His Father. What this sequence shows me is that our God is the God of process. Instead of telling us the answer immediately, He allows time for us to think through, process through, calculate through and realize what He knew before He even asked the question. We can't do this without Him!

In verse 7 we see that Phllip answers and says, *"Two hundred denarii worth of bread would not be enough for each of them to get a little."* In other words, man's strength can only do so much as we see in verse 9.

Have you ever felt that way? You've put all you can into something, given it your all and approached it from every angle but keep coming up short?

There is good news. In II Corinthians 12:9-10 (ESV) Paul writes, *"But he said to me, My grace is sufficient for you, for my power is made perfect in weakness. Therefore I will boast all the more gladly of my weaknesses, so that the power of Christ may rest upon me. For the sake of Christ, then, I am content with weaknesses, insults, hardships, persecutions, and calamities. For when I am weak, then I am strong."*

In this case it took the disciples reaching the end of their rope for Jesus to work His miracle. Aren't you glad that there was a ray of hope in this perplexing situation? In the next verses we see some food is found for this hungry group of people.

In verses 8-10, one of his disciples, Andrew, Simon Peter's brother, said to him, *"There is a boy here who has five barley loaves and two fish, but what are they for so many? Jesus said, 'Have the people sit down.' Now there was much grass in the place. So the men sat down, about five thousand in number. Jesus then took the loaves, and when he had given thanks, he distributed them to those who were seated. So also the fish, as much as they wanted."*

See, the other gospels make it known that the disciples handed out the food as well. But even though they doubted, they were used to distribute.

He also used the boy's lunch. What we see is that He used what the boy had, even though it didn't seem like enough.

Our issue is that many of us are waiting to have a specific amount or be at a specific place before God can use us. Many of us are looking for our gifts to be perfected, but God is saying:
- All I need is willingness.
- All I need is obedience.
- All I need is something to work with.

3) GOD IS MORE AND HAS MORE THAN ENOUGH
After everyone ate their fill the text says, *"And they took up twelve baskets full of broken pieces and of the fish. And those who ate the loaves were five thousand men."* - Mark 6:30-44 (ESV).

The question I have is that if Jesus had more than enough for more than 5,000 men then what makes you think he's lacking enough in your life?

Verse 12 reads, *"And when they had eaten their fill, he told his disciples, 'Gather up the leftover fragments, that nothing may be lost.' So they gathered them up and filled twelve baskets with fragments from the five barley loaves left by those who had eaten."*

They ate their fill. No one had grumbling stomachs after this. It was a complete work. Everything the Lord does, He does well. The question isn't whether or not he can do it. The question is whether or not we have the faith to believe He can. It's about if we have the faith to obey what He says in spite of our present circumstances.

See, Jesus already spoke to them about the kingdom. He did signs, He did miracles and He did wonders. He met their spiritual need. Then the text says He healed them of their infirmities and diseases. God sees your need and is able to provide according to His riches in glory!

Below are some verses to remind and encourage you that God **has** more than enough and **is** more than enough.

- Psalm 103:8-13(ESV) *The LORD is merciful and gracious, slow to anger and abounding in steadfast love. He will not always chide, nor will he keep his anger forever. He does not deal with us according to our sins, nor repay us according to our iniquities. For as high as the heavens are above the earth, so great is his steadfast love toward those who fear him; as far as the east is from the west, so far does he remove our transgressions from us. As a father shows compassion to his children, so the LORD shows compassion to those who fear Him.*

- Romans 8:37-39 (ESV) *No, in all these things we are more than conquerors through him who loved us. For I am sure that neither death nor life, nor angels nor rulers, nor things present nor things to come, nor powers, nor height nor depth, nor anything else in all creation, will be able to separate us from the love of God in Christ Jesus our Lord.*

- Psalm 50:10 (ESV) *For every beast of the forest is mine, the cattle on a thousand hills.*

- Jude 24 (ESV) *Now to him who is able to keep you from stumbling and to present you blameless before the presence of his glory with great joy.*

- Philippians 4:7 (ESV) *And the peace of God, which surpasses all understanding, will guard your hearts and your minds in Christ Jesus.*

- Philippians 4:19 (ESV) *And my God will supply every need of yours according to his riches in glory in Christ Jesus.*

There is a world out there that is hungry, and it may seem like an impossible task to try and feed them but we serve a God Who specializes in the impossible.

We serve a God who has:
> More than enough power!
> More than enough authority!
> More than enough strength!
> More than enough wisdom!

Let's trust Him to be the God who is truly more than enough.

> *"Build me a son, O Lord, who will be strong*
> *enough to know when he is weak, and brave enough*
> *to face himself when he is afraid, and one who will be*
> *proud and unbending in honest defeat,*
> *and humble and gentle in victory."*
> *- Douglas MacArthur -*

THE NUMBER 30
INTERESTING FACTS*

- The number 30 can symbolize dedication to a particular task or calling.

- Aaronic priests were dedicated to serve at 30, in part because it was the age when a person reached both physical and mental maturity and could therefore handle major responsibilities.

- John the Baptist, who was of priestly descent (his mother was a descendant of the daughters of Aaron and his father was a priest), began his ministry at age 30.

- In the Fall of 26 A.D., at the age of 30, Christ began to publicly preach the gospel (Luke 3:23). His ministry lasted for three and one-half years.

- The number thirty can also represent the sacrificial blood of Jesus.

- Christ was betrayed by Judas for 30 silver coins, which was a fulfillment of prophecy (Zechariah 11:12).

- When Judas flung the 'blood money' he was paid back into the temple, the priests did not accept it as an offering but rather decided to buy a potter's field with it. Though they were not aware of it, what they did was also fulfilling prophecy (verse 13).

- In 30 A.D. Jesus suffered and shed His precious blood as God's sacrificial Lamb for the world's sins.

Appearances Of The Number Thirty

- The Dead Sea Scrolls were discovered in caves on the upper northwest shore of the Dead Sea started in 1947. Among all the scrolls found over the years, 30 copies of the Psalms have been identified.

- The patriarchs Salah (grandson of Shem), Peleg (who lived to see the world's continents divide) and Serug (the great-grandfather of Abraham) had their first sons at the age of 30.

- The prophet Ezekiel begins his book of the same name "in the 30th year" (which likely referenced his age at the time - Ezekiel 1:1). It is at this time he receives his first recorded vision from God, known as the "wheel in the middle of a wheel" or "wheel within a wheel" vision.

- Abraham was promised that if God found at least thirty righteous people in Sodom and Gomorrah he would not destroy the cities (Genesis 18:30).

Thirty And The Judges Of Israel

- Jair, one of the Judges of Israel delineated in the Bible, had thirty sons. He was wealthy enough not only to provide each of them with their own horse to ride, but also gave each of them a city (Judges 10:4).

- Ibzan, another Judge of Israel, had thirty sons and thirty daughters (Judges 12:9).

- Samson, a Judge of Israel from 1085 - 1065 B.C., offered a prize of thirty sheets and thirty change of garments to thirty men if they answered a riddle within a week (Judges 14:11 - 14).

How Is The Number 30 Related To Mourning?

- Both the death of Aaron and Moses was mourned by the children of Israel for 30 days (Numbers 20:29, Deuteronomy 34:8).

- Joseph, a type of Jesus, was thirty years old when Egypt's Pharaoh placed him in charge over all that he ruled.

- King David also, when he began to reign over Israel, was thirty years old (Sam 5:4).

*Information gathered from www.biblestudy.org

"Discipline is the soul of an army.
It makes small numbers formidable;
procures success to the weak, and esteem to all."
- George Washington -

ABOUT THE AUTHOR

Beverly Morrison Caesar is the wife of Bishop Roderick R. Caesar, international Bishop of Bethel Gospel Tabernacle. She is an associate pastor of Bethel Gospel Tabernacle in Queens, New York where her son, Rev. Roderick R. Caesar, III is the senior pastor.

Pastor Bev, as she is affectionately called, is an ordained minister in BGT, oversees the women's ministry, heads the Parish Relations team, oversees C.A.R.E. (the small group ministry), and founded & directs the Speech Choir.

She is the founder and director of Arts in Christian Theatre - that produced the blockbuster hit "The Hedge" seen by over 80,000 people. She opened a theatrical training company, ACTStudios. She established a forum for school children to see books that they are reading come alive on stage.

She is an author, penning the manuscript, *Experiencing the 25th Hour.*

Missions was added to her already full portfolio overseeing the local, national and international missions of the BGT ministry. She formed the Veronica Morrison Foundation which functions to provide assistance to an orphanage in Uganda, support Haiti, build houses through Food For The Poor in Jamaica, and donate finances to aid children of Colombo, Sri Lanka.

She obtained her bachelors of science and bachelors of theology degrees from Hunter College and the Bethel Bible Institute, respectively. Beverly is a workshop teacher, seminar conductor, expositor, preacher and teacher of the Word. She also operates in the prophetic.

Pastor Bev resides in Queens with her husband of 40 years. She's the proud mother of three daughters, Naomi Hunter, Lydia Adams, Elizabeth, and their miracle son, Roderick, III. Pastor Bev is the proud grandmother of two granddaughters, Kayliah and Selah Dawn, and a grandson Roderick, IV.

Made in the USA
Middletown, DE
04 March 2021

34851899R00056